BARISTA SECRETS

Creative Coffee at Home

Ryan Soeder and Kohei Matsuno

FIREFLY BOOKS

Contents

Ryan Soeder

I really love coffee, you guys. Coffee is a ritual. We treat it reverently on quiet early mornings and use it as a reason to gather with friends or associates. It gives us fuel in the middle of the day when we need an extra edge, comfort when we need soothing, and, frankly, is just plain delicious.

I've spent the last thirteen years working for some of the best coffee companies in the industry, competing in barista competitions, becoming a coffee educator, and diving into the different aspects that make coffee enjoyable. This, of course, includes ways in which we can make coffee as visually appealing as it is delicious. Namely, latte art.

Latte art is not only hypnotizing to watch and a tremendous amount of fun to practice, but is a promise to the person receiving it— that their drink was made with the utmost care.

It is also a lesson in humility, because it will almost never turn out the way you want it to. When it does go really well, your excitement can only last a moment because it must be handed immediately over to a customer, who may not even look at it.

I'm thrilled to be able to communicate my joy for coffee and latte art in this book. If we find ourselves in the same place at the same time, please say hello, and let's grab a cup of coffee.

Kohei Matsuno

Hi, my name is Kohei Matsuno and I live in Tokyo, Japan. I've won many prizes and accolades for my 3D latte art – including champion of the first "Japanese anime latte art tournament" in 2015.

But, to be honest, my 3D latte art was a by-product of my failure to make free-pouring latte art. However, instead of giving up, I decided to get creative and play with the leftover milk foam. At that time, no one knew how to make solid milk foam stand on top of a latte, so the first few cups were time-consuming and ugly. After countless trials and errors, I managed to turn milk foam into cute animals and objects. And now, more than 3,000 cups later, I perform on TV and have a following of coffee lovers from all over the world.

My work is inspired by movies, fine art, fashion, celebrities, and cartoons, and I love bringing joyful surprises and smiles to audiences young and old.

I'm delighted that 3D latte art is one of the newest and most exciting coffee trends, and that baristas across the world are bringing a whole new dimension to coffee.

FREE POURING

Free pouring (see pages 38–59) is where the real skill is. This is what the professional baristas do. Hearts, tulips, swans, and much more.

The spacing of the layers in **Jibbi Little's** free-pour tulip is fascinating.

Ian Chagunda introduces an incredible number of layers to this free-pour tulip design.

A lovely example of the kind of fun to be had with rippled and solid free-pour tulip layers by **Alan Chan.**

A unique take on multiple rosettas by **Simeon Bricker.**

ETCHING

Etching (see pages 60-75) involves drawing into the frothy
surface. Some baristas use syrup or chocolate fudge sauce
to coax out the design.

Michael Breach uses
multiple cups to create
this etched bicycle.

This charming design by **Kohei
Matsuno** uses chocolate sauce to
create the cat, the espresso for
the shadow, and clean lines to
draw the cup.

Kohei Matsuno's fun design brings a new meaning to losing yourself in a cup of coffee.

A stunning etching reproduction of Van Gogh's Starry Night by **Kohei Matsuno.**

ETCHING & FREE POURING

Combining free pouring and etching brings the best
elements of each to the cup – the flow of free pour
and the detail

A fancy free-pour swan
dressed up with etching
details by **Simeon Bricker.**

Jibbi Little uses a
combination of free-pour
and etching techniques to
create this splendid beast.

ETCHING & COLORWORK

By introducing syrups and food colorings to your etching designs, you open up a whole world of latte-art possibilities.

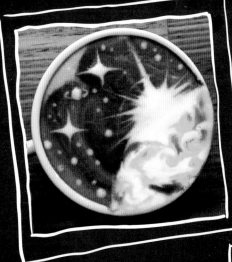

When we say that, with etching, the world is your oyster, few people take that more seriously than **Yuichi Ito "Belcorno."**

Nowtoo Sugi uses etching techniques to reproduce The Great Wave off Kanagawa by Katsushika Hokusai.

FOAM SCULPTURE

Get three-dimensional and create real impact with foam sculptures that jump right out of the cup (see pages 76–95)!

The legs of **Kohei Matsuno's** octopus reach out and over the edge of the cup.

Nowtoo Sugi's shark leaps up and out at the drinker!

It doesn't get more adorable than this! Use 3D sculpture techniques to add the highest level of cute to your drink. Great job, **Nowtoo Sugi.**

Nowtoo Sugi reaches new heights of foam in this giraffe sculpture.

CHAPTER ONE

BARISTA

BASICS

Just like a painter has to learn how to mix colors and prepare a canvas before they can start to paint, you must first learn to pull delicious espresso and steam perfectly textured milk. Latte art can only be as good as the quality of its parts, so if your milk is bubbly and thick, or the espresso is watery and thin, it doesn't matter how well you pour. But with creamy milk and rich, dark espresso, beautiful latte art almost pours itself!

BASIC TECHNIQUES

Remember, your first obligation is to serve someone a great tasting as well as a great looking drink.

CHOOSE A PITCHER

All of the designs in this book can be poured with a spouted pitcher. Begin by filling the pitcher with milk out of the refrigerator. Measure the amount of milk you need by filling the cup you're going to pour into and put that into the pitcher. The liquid should end up just under the halfway point of the pitcher. If the pitcher is more than half full it will be very difficult to steam without spilling. If it's less than a quarter of the way full it will be difficult to control the aeration process and create well-textured milk.

PULL A SHOT OF ESPRESSO

Begin by grinding fresh coffee into the portafilter basket so that it forms a centered mound. Flatten the pile, brush off the excess coffee, then press it down evenly with a tamper. It is important to press all the air out of the coffee grounds and give the water an even path through the puck of coffee. If there are inconsistencies in the bed of coffee or the tamp is uneven, the pressurized water from the grouphead will find those weak points and shoot through them, creating thin, watery, bitter espresso.

MAKE ADJUSTMENTS

Lock in the portafilter and press the brew button. The goal is a shot of espresso that takes between 25–30 seconds to reach 1½–2 oz (45–60 ml) in volume. If it takes more than 30 seconds to reach 1½ oz (45 ml), make the grind coarser, so the water flows faster with less resistance from the grounds. If it takes less than 25 seconds to reach 2 oz (60 ml), make the grind finer so the coffee grounds provide more resistance and slow down the shot. Once you are within range, decide whether you want the shot to be thicker or thinner. A 1½ oz (45 ml) espresso will have more body and viscosity than a 2 oz (60 ml) espresso, and the longer it takes to reach the desired volume, the more developed and aggressive the espresso will taste.

Once the coffee is level, press it down evenly with a tamper until the coffee pushes back.

Press all the air out of the coffee grounds to give the water an even path through the puck of coffee.

STEAM MILK FOR LATTE ART

1 Begin with the tip of the steam wand completely submerged below the surface of the milk. Place the steam wand in the spout of the pitcher and tilt the pitcher to the side so that the steam wand is submerged off-center, halfway between the center and the wall of the pitcher.

2 Turn the steam wand all the way on, place your hand on the side of the pitcher to feel the temperature of the milk, and lower the pitcher so that the steam wand begins to pull air into the milk through the downward force of steam. Keep note of the temperature and do not add any air after the milk starts to feel warm. Aerating after this point will result in stiff foam that is hard to work with.

3 Proper aeration should hiss steadily like the sound of paper tearing. If it only chirps intermittently, pull down slightly on the pitcher to add more air. If it sounds like TV static and bubbles up, lift the pitcher slightly to aerate less.

4 To stop aerating, close the gap between the surface of the milk and the tip of the steam wand. At this point the steam wand should still be spinning the milk in a spiral but no longer making any aeration noises. Keep this position until the pitcher is too hot to touch with your hand.

5 Turn off the steam wand, set the pitcher aside, and immediately turn the steam back on for one second to purge any milk from the inside while you clean the outside with a damp cloth.

6 After steaming there may be a few visible bubbles floating in the rich, shiny foam. Simply tap the pitcher on the counter to pop those bubbles and swirl the milk in the pitcher to polish the foam into a smooth, homogenous texture. Keep swirling the milk until pouring so that it doesn't separate into a foam layer on top and liquid on the bottom. The result should look like marshmallow fluff or wet paint.

Place the steam wand in the spout of the pitcher, and tilt the pitcher to the side so that the steam wand is submerged off-center.

Turn the steam wand all the way on and place your hand on the side of the pitcher to feel the temperature.

BASIC PRINCIPLES

Now that you've prepared a nice, dark espresso to work as a canvas, and perfectly textured milk to act as paint, you can combine the two. Just like painting, it's important to learn the principles behind different brushstrokes before you start making portraits.

MILK THICKNESS

The amount of air you inject into the milk during steaming will determine how thick or thin the foam in the pitcher will be. Thinner milk will flow freely and look wispy, while thicker milk will look more bold and solid.

HEIGHT

The distance between the spout of the pitcher and the surface of the liquid in the cup determines when the design will appear. The first part of every pour begins with filling the cup about halfway while keeping the pitcher at least 1½ in. (3 cm) above the drink. This will allow the foam to fall through the liquid in the cup, keeping anything from showing up before you're ready. Once the cup is half full, tilt it so that the liquid is right at the edge and lower the pitcher so that the spout is less than ½ in. (1 cm) away. This will cause the foam to float across the surface and begin to create the design.

FLOW RATE

Pouring too quickly can cause you to lose control of the design, while pouring too slowly can cause the lines of a design to clump together. As you fill the cup with foam, you increase the surface tension in the cup so, generally, pour slower at the beginning of a design when tension is low and pick up the pace toward the end as surface tension increases.

POSITION

Where you place the spout of the pitcher when you pour determines what kinds of lines form and where they travel. Pouring in the center will cause lines to travel toward the bottom of the cup, then curl back up toward the pitcher, forming a circle. Pouring toward one side or the other will cause the foam to spiral around the cup.

Practice your pace! Start by pouring slowly and speed up as you finish your design.

Tilting the cup and pouring the milk close to the edge will help the foam float across the surface.

Start pouring with the pitcher 1½ in. (3 cm) above the drink and lower the spout to ½ in. (1 cm) from the drink when creating your design.

Think about the position of your pour, since pouring in the center or toward one side will affect the style and direction of the pattern you're forming.

The first part of every pour involves filling the cup with milk to an imaginary marker.

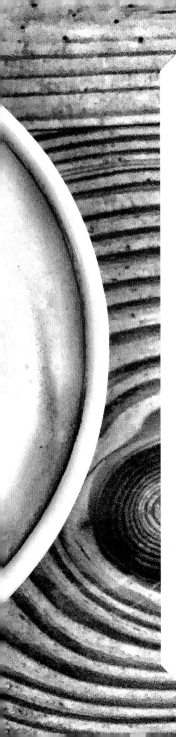

CHAPTER TWO

USING STENCILS

The easiest, most repeatable, and (arguably) most delicious way to make designs in a latte is to use a stencil and flavored powder. You can make a stencil for any occasion or create themed or personalized designs for friends or special gatherings. Stencils can be kept and reused, so you can bring them out season after season, or you can modify your old stencils to keep them fresh and engaging.

WHAT POWDERS?

Because taste should be your first priority, choosing a powder that complements the flavor of the espresso drink is vital. You can have a lot of fun (and get very caffeinated!) playing around with different flavor combinations. Here are some classic combinations to get you started

Discovering fantastic new flavors to highlight old favorites is half the fun of decorating with powders, so head to the grocery store, load up on flavors, and don't be afraid to get weird!

DRINK	POWDER
HOT CHOCOLATE/MOCHA	CITRUS PEEL, COCOA, CAYENNE
CARAMEL LATTE	SEA SALT, BURNT SUGAR, COCOA
CHAI LATTE	CLOVES, CINNAMON, CARDAMOM
LATTE	BURNT SUGAR, COCOA
EARL GREY LATTE	CITRUS PEEL, COCOA

HOT CHOCOLATE/MOCHA

CITRUS PEEL

COCOA

CAYENNE

CARAMEL LATTE

SEA SALT

BURNT SUGAR

COCOA

CHAI LATTE

CLOVES

CINNAMON

CARDAMOM

LATTE

BURNT SUGAR

COCOA

EARL GREY LATTE

CITRUS PEEL

COCOA

USING STENCILS

The main thing to consider when using powders and stencils is achieving flavor balance while maintaining good contrast of the design.

You want to use enough powder to make the design stand out, but you don't want the flavor of the powder to take over the entire drink. Remember that the design should accent the drink, not become the entire point of the drink. Also, no one wants to be chewing on grit while they're trying to enjoy their beverage.

The trick is to get the stencil as close to the surface of the drink as possible without dipping it into the foam, and gently tapping out the powder from about 6 in. (15 cm) above the stencil. Keeping the stencil close to the drink ensures crisp edges and good definition of the design, while tapping out the powder from as high over the drink as possible allows the air between the shaker and the stencil to break up any clumps as the powder falls. The easiest way to do this is to slightly underfill the cup so you can rest the stencil directly on the lip. Be sure to use a mat or saucer under the cup to avoid any potential powder stains on the countertop.

MAKE YOUR OWN STENCILS

You can buy pre-made stencils, but half the fun of dressing up a drink in this way is making your own!

You can use any number of materials. Paper is great for one-off designs. For instance, you can make snowflakes by folding paper in half or quarters and cutting fractal designs into it like you did when you were a kid in school. This method also works well for Art Deco or stained glass-style patterns.

If you want longer-lasting stencils, you can use a sturdier material, such as a thin sheet of plastic. Use scissors to cut a circle slightly larger than the cup, then use a craft knife to cut the design in the circle. This takes longer than folding and cutting paper, but gives greater design freedom.

Try not to include too many large holes in your design in order to prevent using too much flavored powder. For instance, cutting a large, solid heart out of the middle of your stencil would cover most of the surface of the drink with grit. Instead, try cutting just the outline or using intersecting, layered rings, so you get the idea across without using too much powder. The designs opposite give an idea of the possibilities.

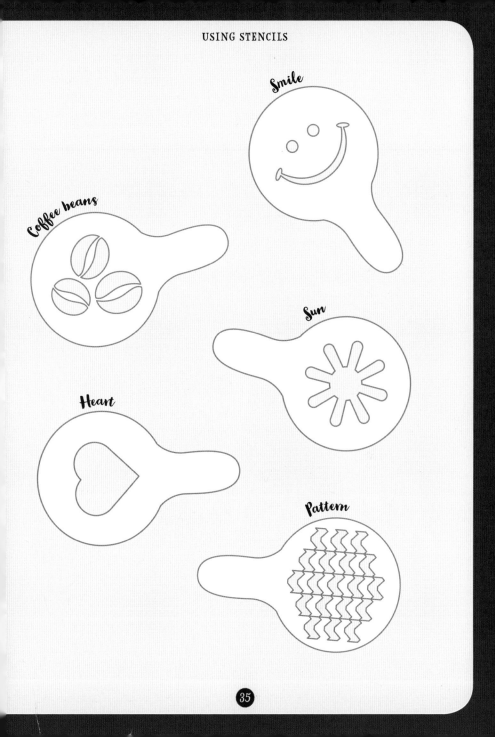

Smile

Coffee beans

Sun

Heart

Pattern

CHAPTER THREE

FREE POURING

The designs you can create by simply pouring milk into coffee are incredible - hearts, tulips, swans, and much more! All you need is some dark espresso coffee, some white creamy milk, a pitcher, and a steady hand. Learn the basic designs, then start combining or improvising with them to create your own unique cups of coffee.

ALL ABOUT
Free Pouring

Free-pour latte art is the style of
professional baristas, largely
because it takes no longer to make
the design than it would to pour the
drink without it.

The longer a drink sits on the counter, the worse it's going to taste, and using free pour is the only way to simultaneously make a beautiful design while safeguarding every bit of deliciousness in the cup. The fact that it happens so quickly, and that there is no way to fix the design once it's in the cup, makes free pour the most difficult style to master—and the most beautiful when it goes well.

Every free-pour design begins by tilting the cup and filling it to the rim from at least 1½ in. (3 cm) above the cup. This will bring the liquid in the cup to a point where you can lower the pitcher to the rim and begin making a crisp, white design without accidentally drawing anything before you're ready. Once the cup is filled to the rim, break the stream of milk, touch the spout of the pitcher to the rim of the cup to bring the spout within ½ in. (1 cm) of the liquid in the cup, and begin the design. Every design element from this point on will occur while the pitcher is touching the cup.

Solid Heart

This design teaches all the basic free-pouring movements with no extra frills to complicate things. Although simple, it is immediately recognizable and is sure to impress.

Pour very slowly just above the center of the liquid in the cup until the edges of the heart meet at the spout of the pitcher.

Increase the flow rate to fill the inside of the heart. Move the pitcher forward slightly with this higher flow rate.

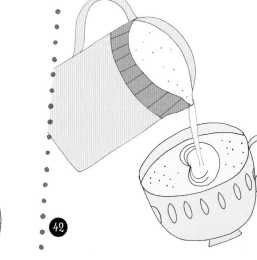

SOLID HEART

3
When the cup is nearly full, raise the pitcher to about 1½ in. (3 cm) above the liquid to stop forming the design.

4
Move the pitcher to the bottom of the heart to form the tail.

Rippled Heart

The rippled heart is a variation on the solid heart (see page 42), but with added rings and texture. The perfect design to prepare for someone you love.

Pour at a moderate speed just above the center of the liquid in the cup.

Move the pitcher from side to side slightly so the milk in the pitcher rocks back and forth but the pitcher itself doesn't move too much. This will cause the stream of milk to form rings.

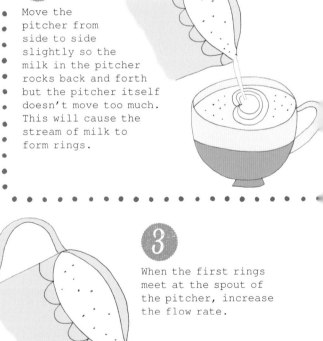

When the first rings meet at the spout of the pitcher, increase the flow rate.

4

Move the pitcher forward slightly with this higher flow rate.

5

When the cup is nearly full, stop rocking the pitcher and raise it to 1½ in. (3 cm) above the liquid in the cup to stop forming the design. Move the pitcher to the bottom of the heart to create the tail.

Rosetta

The rosetta is one of the most difficult designs to pull
off because it involves many movements, poured with
precision, in a very short amount of time. A good rosetta
should fill the cup, be entirely symmetrical, and have
gaps between every leaf.

1 Pour with a medium-high
flow rate in the center of
the liquid in the cup.

2 Move the
pitcher from
side to side
to rock the
milk inside
the pitcher.

3 When the ripples meet at
the spout of the pitcher,
increase the flow rate
slightly and move the
pitcher to the top of the
cup as you continue to rock
the milk.

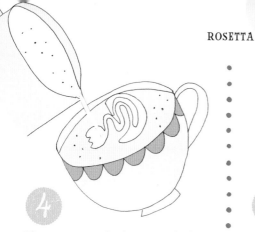

4 When you reach the top of the cup, stop moving the pitcher and decrease the flow rate to form a solid heart at the top.

5 With a very low flow rate, lift the pitcher straight up over the heart to 1½ in. (3 cm) above the liquid in the cup.

6 Keeping a low flow rate, slowly move through the center of the design toward the bottom of the cup to draw the leaves of the rosetta together.

Basic Tulip

Tulips are a lot of fun to pour because there are many variations to play around with and they provide the opportunity to fix any symmetry mistakes as you form the layers. A good way to think about a tulip is as hearts stacked on top of each other.

1. Pour with a medium-high flow rate in the center of the liquid in the cup, rocking the milk in the pitcher. When the ripples meet at the spout of the pitcher, move the pitcher forward slightly and stop pouring.

2. Reposition the pitcher so that the spout is in the top half of the cup and pour a solid heart (see page 42) just above the rippled base.

3. When the cup is nearly full, raise the pitcher to 1½ in. (3 cm) above the liquid in the cup to stop forming the design. Move the pitcher to the bottom of the heart to form the tail.

ADDING LAYERS

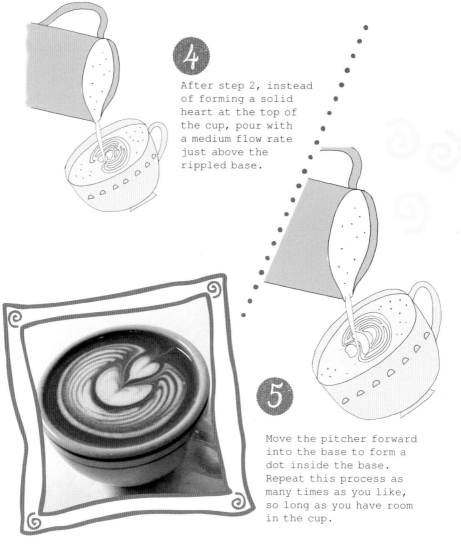

4

After step 2, instead of forming a solid heart at the top of the cup, pour with a medium flow rate just above the rippled base.

5

Move the pitcher forward into the base to form a dot inside the base. Repeat this process as many times as you like, so long as you have room in the cup.

Multiple Rosettas

Once you're comfortable with different flow rates, forming ripples, moving around the cup, and stopping and starting to add layers, you can have a lot of fun combining different designs to create new versions.

1 Pour in the center of the cup with a very low flow rate. Move the pitcher from side to side quickly to create small ripples.

2 Immediately move the pitcher forward to the top of the cup so the first rosetta doesn't spread too much.

3 When you reach the top of the cup, raise the pitcher to 1½ in. (3 cm) above the liquid in the cup to stop forming the design.

5

Stop pouring
when you reach
the bottom
of the cup.

4

Slowly move the pitcher
through the design to draw
the leaves together.

6

Repeat this process on either
side of the first rosetta.
Keep in mind that surface
tension is increasing as you
fill the cup, so each
additional rosetta will
require a higher flow rate and
a more exaggerated motion of
the pitcher to achieve
good definition.

Swan

Pouring a recognizable figure like a swan is a double-edged sword. On one hand, people go nuts when they see a design they can identify. On the other, it's painfully obvious when something goes wrong. Be sure to practice — being able to blow friends and family away with this design is well worth the time it takes to master it.

1 Begin with a single rosetta (see page 46) to the side of the cup. Pour with a very low flow rate but move the pitcher from side to side quickly to create small ripples. Use a very low flow rate and pull back immediately to the top of the cup.

2 When you reach the top of the cup, raise the pitcher to 1½ in. (3 cm) above the liquid in the cup to stop forming the design.

3 Instead of moving the pitcher through the center of the rosetta, move the stream of milk along the side closest to the center of the cup. Draw the leaves together along that edge to form the wing of the swan.

SWAN

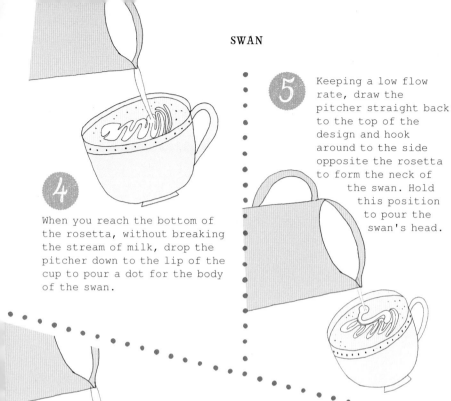

5 Keeping a low flow rate, draw the pitcher straight back to the top of the design and hook around to the side opposite the rosetta to form the neck of the swan. Hold this position to pour the swan's head.

4 When you reach the bottom of the rosetta, without breaking the stream of milk, drop the pitcher down to the lip of the cup to pour a dot for the body of the swan.

6 When the head is complete, lift the pitcher back up to 1½ in. (3 cm) above the surface of the liquid in the cup and pour through the solid heart to form the beak.

Wreath

Create this pretty design by pouring
an asymmetric rosetta that wraps around
the cup. It doesn't matter if it's not
precision perfect—play this one fast
and loose.

1

Pour fast along one of
the sides to spin the
liquid in the cup. When
the liquid reaches the
lip of the cup, drop
the pitcher down to
begin the design.

2

Pour a rosetta (see page 46)
along the side of the cup at a
high flow rate, moving the
pitcher quickly from side to
side to create small ripples.

WREATH

3

When the cup is almost
full, move the pitcher to
the top of the design as
you would with a rosetta.

4

When you reach the top of
the design, raise the pitcher
to 1½ in. (3 cm) above the
liquid in the cup to stop
forming the design. With a
low flow rate, pour through
the center of the rosetta to
draw the leaves together.

Hanging Heart

The hanging heart is a bucket of fun. It doesn't make a lot of sense and it doesn't need to. This design combines elements in such a way as to make it look like a solid heart is hung from a wreath.

1 Pour at a fast flow rate along one side of the cup to spin the liquid.

2 Drop the pitcher down to the lip of the cup to pour a rosetta (see page 46) that wraps around the cup.

4 Once the heart is complete, raise the pitcher to 1½ in. (3 cm) above the liquid to stop forming the design. Move the pitcher to the bottom of the heart to create the tail.

3 When the rosetta has wrapped around the cup, pull back to the top of the design but, instead of drawing the leaves together (see page 42), form a solid heart (see page 42) in the center without breaking the stream.

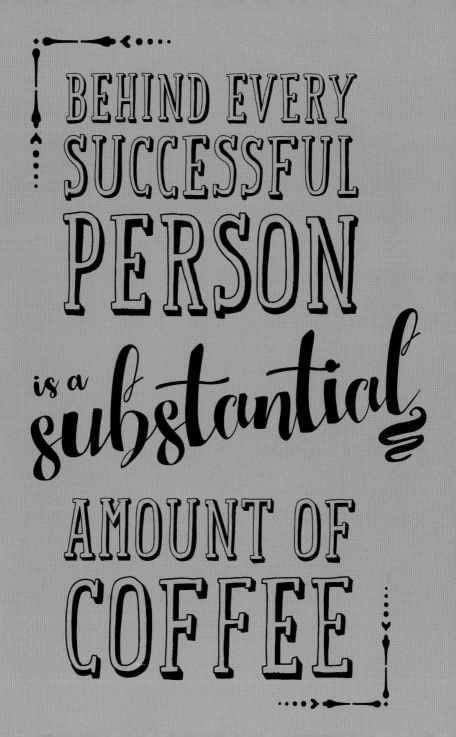

CHAPTER FOUR

ETCHING

Etching involves drawing in the frothy surface with a pointed implement. You can create simple geometric patterns that require no artistic skill and really are the work of moments, or you can recreate the work of the old masters in coffee form. Add chocolate or caramel sauce to further enhance your designs and add a sweetness to the drink.

ALL ABOUT
ETCHING

Etching takes longer than free pouring, so you don't see it as often behind busy coffee bars. It does, however, really let you use your imagination and create anything you can think of in the cup. Etching techniques are perfect for adding little details to free-pour art, or for making your own creations from scratch at home.

You'll need a few things to get started. In order to manipulate the foam on the top of the drink, you'll need a long, pointed tool. Milk thermometers work well for this, because they're handy to have around anyway in order to check drink temperatures, and are the perfect thickness for this kind of work. All kinds of other pointy objects will work, though, like a large toothpick (make sure it's not minty!), a tiny glasses screw driver, a pointy chopstick, an ice pick, etc.

You'll also need a pointed squeezy bottle if you want to use a sauce like chocolate or caramel to create designs. This will help control the application of the sauce and let you choose exactly how and where to place it on the surface of the foam.

Another thing to have handy is a towel to wipe the pointy tool clean in between foam manipulations. Every time you move the foam, you'll be left with the color of the part of the drink you moved on the tool. Clean the tool every time it touches the drink to avoid adding color to the wrong place.

Be sure to have all of the materials close by to use as soon as you're ready. It's no good having the drink degrading on the counter while you look for something you forgot.

It's important to note that, if you're using espresso to pour into, the dark cream on the surface of the drink will swallow any sauce you apply, so pour the entire design with the spout close to the surface of the drink and accept a lot of beige, ghostly colors in order to provide enough foam on top of the drink to support the sauce. If, however, you're making a hot chocolate, chai, or anything that doesn't use espresso, feel free to make the design as crisp and clear as you like.

Embellishing with Sauce

Embellishing a free-pour design is a great way to get used to applying sauces to a drink in a controlled way and to practice the different kinds of motions required to manipulate the design.

1 Pour a solid heart (see page 42) or any design you like.

(see page 42)

2 Draw a line along each side of the heart with sauce, starting from the bottom of the cup.

3 Using your etching tool, swirl in a counterclockwise direction, as if you were drawing a spring, along the line of sauce on the right-hand side of the drink.

4 Repeat, swirling in a clockwise direction, along the line of sauce on the left-hand side of the drink.

Stars with Sauce

Create a star pattern using nothing but chocolate sauce!
Once you've mastered this basic technique, you can create
many more complex designs by improvising.

1 Using chocolate sauce, draw a small circle, about 1 in. (2.5 cm) wide, in the middle of the cup. Then draw another circle about ½ in. (1 cm) outside the first.

2 Starting from the center of the circles, drag the etching tool straight out to the edge of the cup, lifting slightly so as not to submerge the design.

3 Repeat step 2 for each point on the compass: N, E, S, and W.

Find a place between any two points. Starting from the edge of the cup, drag the etching tool into the center of the circles.

Repeat step 4 for each intermediate point on the compass: NE, SE, SW, and NW.

Place the etching tool in the center of the circles to gather each of the internal points. Lift it straight up and out of the drink to make the points meet in the center.

Line Swirls

This is a very easy, but very impressive-looking design. People will spend time trying to figure out how it's done, not realizing how simple it is.

LINE SWIRLS

1 Using sauce, draw as many lines as you like across the surface of the drink.

2 Place the etching tool in the drink at the top of the cup and drag it straight down through the lines.

3 When you reach the bottom of the cup, without removing the etching tool from the drink, make a U-turn and drag it straight up through the lines next to the downstroke. Repeat until you reach the end of the lines.

4 Lift the etching tool as you approach the edge of the cup to draw the design to a point.

Butterfly

Etching recognizable shapes is a tremendous amount of fun because people love designs they're familiar with. The butterfly is a great etching design because there's no way to replicate it with any other technique, and it looks much more complicated than it really is.

1 Follow steps 1–3 of the solid heart (page 42) and continue pouring until the cup is full. This will create a dimpled dot in the center. Dip the etching tool into the middle of the dot to pick up white foam.

2 Starting near the top of the cup and slightly off-center, drag the etching tool down into the center of the dot to create each antenna.

3 Place the etching tool in the upper corners of the dot and drag upward and outward to the edge of the cup to create the top wing tips.

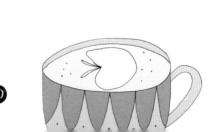

BUTTERFLY

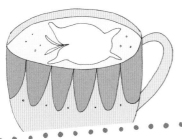

4 Place the etching tool in the lower corners of the dot and drag downward and outward to the edge of the cup to create the bottom wing tips.

6

Place the etching tool below the dot, just inside the two bottom wing tips, and drag almost to the center of the dot to form the body.

5 Starting at the edge of the cup in the SE and SW positions, drag the etching tool in upward arcs almost to the center of the dot to separate the upper and lower wings.

Teddy Bear

This little guy is just adorable. Incorporating free-pour and etching techniques, this design is perfect for kids' hot chocolates.

Follow steps 1-3 of the solid heart (page 42). When the edges of the design meet at the tip of the spout, stop pouring to form the head.

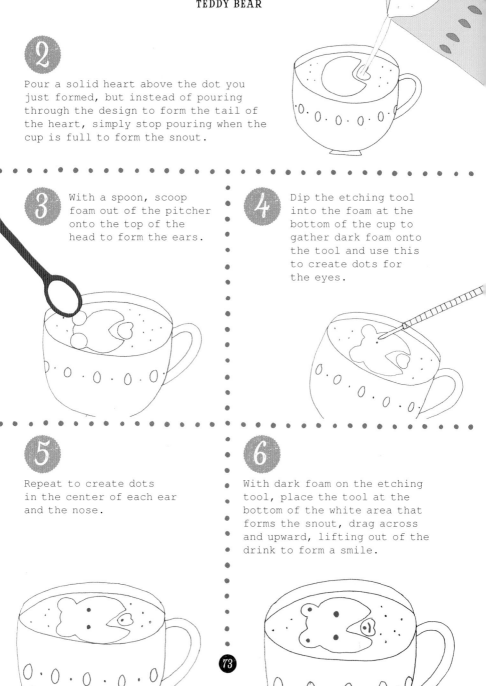

2

Pour a solid heart above the dot you just formed, but instead of pouring through the design to form the tail of the heart, simply stop pouring when the cup is full to form the snout.

3

With a spoon, scoop foam out of the pitcher onto the top of the head to form the ears.

4

Dip the etching tool into the foam at the bottom of the cup to gather dark foam onto the tool and use this to create dots for the eyes.

5

Repeat to create dots in the center of each ear and the nose.

6

With dark foam on the etching tool, place the tool at the bottom of the white area that forms the snout, drag across and upward, lifting out of the drink to form a smile.

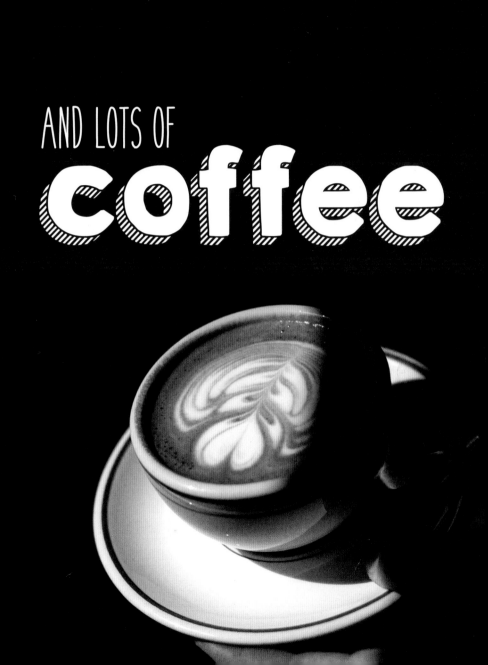

AND LOTS OF

coffee

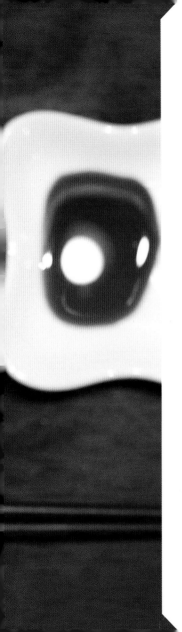

CHAPTER FIVE

3D FOAM SCULPTURE

3D foam sculptures bring a special "wow" to a regular cup of coffee, and now you can make them, too! First, master the art of making "silky" and "coarse" foam, explained on page 70, then sculpt away. Drawing in the foam with syrup will add the final details to your mini masterpieces.

ALL ABOUT
3D FOAM
Sculpture

The biggest difference between 2D and 3D latte art is, of course, the shaping and characteristics of the milk foam: 2D art uses small, dense, smooth foam, which we call "silky," whereas 3D art uses big, bulky, lightweight foam, which we call "coarse."

The lightweight coarse foam used for 3D latte art dissolves faster than dense silky foam, meaning that delivering a 3D foam sculpture requires you to be quick and agile. It also means that the lifespan of your artworks is limited, making them a truly one-of-a-kind creation.

The technique for making silky foam is described on page 22. To make the coarse foam required for 3D sculptures, you need to aerate the milk as you steam it. Leave a little more of a gap between the wand and the milk than you would do normally, and listen for a "tss tss" sound. Stir the milk after steaming, then leave it to stand for about a minute. The liquid will separate into two layers: the milk will settle at the bottom and the foam on top will be hard and light, perfect for 3D sculpture.

A few tools are useful for 3D foam sculpture. A couple of spoons can be used to place and design foam on top of the coffee, and any kind of pick (metal or wooden) with a fine point can be used to draw on the latte, like a pen.

Hello Bunny

Creating the ears of this rabbit can be challenging, however, you can try again a number of times, as long as you have sufficient foam. Make sure to add supporting foam wherever required, for example, for the face or the ears.

1 Take a scoop of coarse foam and place it against the edge of the cup to begin building the rabbit's head. Continue adding foam on top of this until you have the size you want.

3 Add small portions of foam to the first shape to create ears. This can be challenging as you are dealing with taller shapes. Start with a small base for support and build on top of it slowly.

2 Add a smaller ball of foam to one side of the head to form the rabbit's waving hand.

5 Add a small rectangle of foam to the front of the cup—this is where you can add a personalized message.

4 Use a teaspoon to draw the foam upward to form taller, more pointed ears.

6 Use picks covered in chocolate sauce and red syrup to draw the face of the rabbit and the details, such as the inside of the ears, then add a message.

Animal Party

When combining 3D latte art with written messages, it's important to do all of the 3D work first, since the linework can begin to smear or dissolve more quickly. There is a lot of illustration work in this project, so make sure you get a good coating of silky foam over the initial shapes, since this will last longer and be easier to draw on.

Use a pair of spoons to create the rough shapes of the animals from coarse foam, placing them around the cup, leaving a space in the front.

Use the spoons to gently coat the animals with silky foam, taking care not to break their shapes.

Add small pieces of coarse foam to the existing shapes to create ears and noses, using the spoons to gently pull them into shape.

Use picks coated with chocolate sauce and red syrup to add details to each of the characters. Add a personal message as a finishing touch.

Classic Car

The coating process—covering the coarse foam shape with a layer of silky foam—creates a beautiful curve that allows the details of your design to stand out. This project is perfect for practicing this technique.

1 Using a pair of spoons, add a large rectangle of coarse foam to the center of the cup for the base of the car.

2 Add more foam on top of the center of the rectangle to build up the windshield and roof of the car.

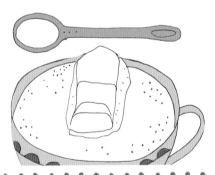

3 Now cover the whole design with silky foam, using the back of a teaspoon to gently carve out your ideal shape.

4 Using a pick covered in chocolate sauce, draw in the details of the car: the tires, windows, and doors. Include as much or as little detail as you like, but try to work quickly, since the foam will start to dissolve after a little while.

Napping Pandas

If you're dealing with a lot of foam, start with less coffee in the cup, so it doesn't spill. This cute panda design can be challenging, because you need to keep the two characters distinct. You should also be careful during the coloring step to avoid smearing the rest of the cup.

1

Create the mother panda first using a pair of spoons to place and shape scoops of coarse foam in the center of the cup.

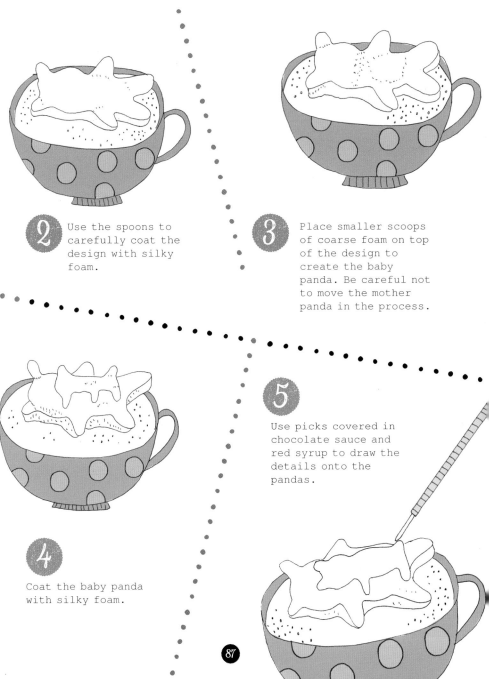

2 Use the spoons to carefully coat the design with silky foam.

3 Place smaller scoops of coarse foam on top of the design to create the baby panda. Be careful not to move the mother panda in the process.

5 Use picks covered in chocolate sauce and red syrup to draw the details onto the pandas.

4 Coat the baby panda with silky foam.

Snowman

The challenge for the snowman is stacking layers of foam on top of each other. This is quite difficult, because the second layer requires a strong base to hold its shape on top.

 Using coarse foam and a pair of spoons, place a small ball in the center of the cup as the base of the snowman's body.

Encase this ball in another layer of foam to build up the body—just like building a real snowman!

Add a small ball of coarse foam on top of the body to begin building the head.

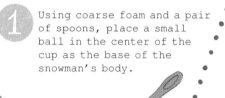

Repeat step 2 with the head, adding another layer to develop the shape.

 Use picks covered in chocolate sauce and red syrup to draw on the details of the snowman and his accessories.

5 Use a teaspoon to gently shape the top ball into a slightly triangular shape—this will be the snowman's hat.

Boat

Adding more depth to the 2D aspects of the design will make the 3D sculpture stand out more so use your imagination in both areas to create a beautiful cup of latte art.

1 Use a spoon to spread silky foam across two thirds of the surface of the coffee.

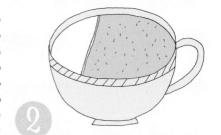

2 Fill this area with blue curacao syrup to create the sea.

3 Use a pick to add dots of chocolate sauce in the brown area to create sand.

4 Using a pair of teaspoons, take one scoop of coarse foam and create a boat shape from this in the center of the cup.

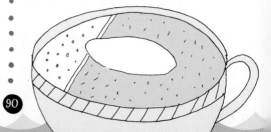

6

Use a teaspoon to shape the boat, then add details with a pick covered with chocolate sauce. The boat may not stay in shape for very long, so try to move quickly from this point.

5

With a teaspoon, coat the boat shape with silky foam to create a smooth surface. If the white foam spills into the blue area you can always fix it with more syrup.

7

Add some foam with a pick to the sea to finalize your piece.

Mount Fuji

It's not difficult to form the basic shape of the mountain, so focus on the coloring process to create a beautiful 3D sculpture.

1 Use a pair of teaspoons to add coarse foam to the center of the cup to create the basic shape of a mountain.

2 Scoop silky foam from the pitcher with a spoon and pour it over the mountain to smooth out the silhouette.

3

Apply a light layer of coffee from the cup to the mountain. Use the back of a teaspoon to hold the foam in shape and in position as you work.

5 Place an extra dollop of foam onto the top of the mountain with a spoon to form a snowy summit.

4 Add color to the mountain by pouring blue curacao syrup over the base with a spoon.

6 Create a winding path down the mountain by dipping a toothpick in some foam and gently dragging it down the side of the sculpture.

93

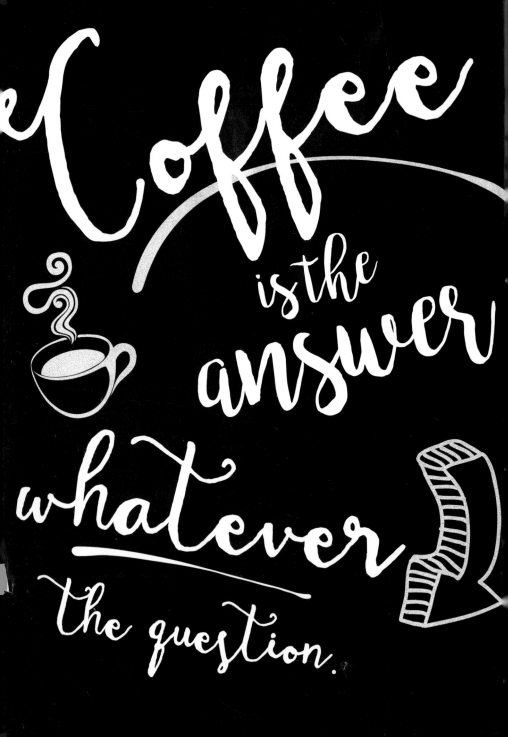

A FIREFLY BOOK

Published by Firefly Books Ltd. 2017

First printing

Publisher Cataloging-in-Publication Data (U.S.)

Names: Soeder, Ryan, author. | Matsuno, Kohei, author.
Title: Barista Secrets : Creative Coffee at Home /Ryan Soeder and
    Kohei Matsuno.
Description: Richmond Hill, Ontario, Canada : Firefly Books, 2017. |
    Summary: "Two professional baristas show how to make artistic
    specialty coffee using foam and milk to create designs in the top
    of the cup. Features a photo gallery of latte art, including coloured
    foam sculptures, by the award-winning authors" – Provided by
    publisher.
Identifiers: ISBN 978-1-77085-914-2 (hardcover)
Subjects: LCSH: Coffee drinks. | Food presentation.
Classification: LCC TX817.C6S643 |DDC 641.3373 – dc23

Library and Archives Canada Cataloguing in Publication

Soeder, Ryan, author
    Barista secrets : creative coffee at home / Ryan Soeder and
Kohei Matsuno.
ISBN 978-1-77085-914-2 (hardcover)
    1. Coffee. 2. Coffee brewing. I. Matsuno, Kohei, author II.
Title.
TX817.C6S64 2017   641.3'373   C2017-900135-3

Published in the United States by
Firefly Books (U.S.) Inc.
P.O. Box 1338, Ellicott Station
Buffalo, New York 14205

Published in Canada by
Firefly Books Ltd.
50 Staples Avenue, Unit 1
Richmond Hill, Ontario L4B 0A7

Printed in China

MIX
Paper from
responsible sources
FSC
www.fsc.org   **FSC® C104723**

CREDITS

Quarto would like to thank the following artists for supplying images for inclusion in this book:

Breach, Michael, www.baristart. com p.12cl; Bricker, Simeon, www.simeondavid.com pp.11br, 14tcr; Chang, Alan, www. oneorigin.com.au p.11tl; Chagunda, Ian, www. ianchagunda p.10bl; Ito, Yuichi "BELCORNO", www.belcorno.jp p.15c; Little, Jibbi, www.jibbijug. com pp.10cr, 14bl; Matsuno, Kohei, p.12br, 13, 16cl; Sugi, Nowtoo, instagram.com/Nowtoo pp.15br, 16br, 17; Happy Monkey, Shutterstock.com p.9; Isselle, Eric, Shutterstock.com p.26; hello/Stockimo/Alamy p28; aerolatte© p33; Mr_Sonis/ iStockphoto.com p.37; Towndrow, Lee, Getty Images p.95; Wongchana, Siriwat, Shutterstock.com p.60

All step-by-step and other images are the copyright of Quarto Publishing plc. While every effort has been made to credit contributors, Quarto would like to apologize should there have been any omissions or errors—and would be pleased to make the appropriate correction for future editions of the book.